On Pressure Washers

E. K. Jones

Copyright © 2017 by E. K. Jones.

All rights reserved. This book and any portion therein or thereof may not be reproduced in any manner without the express written consent of the publisher, except for the purposes of a book review.

Table of Contents

INTRODUCTION 5
HOW THEY WORK 9
USES 13
MAINTENANCE 18
REPAIR 20
WHAT'S NEXT 23

Introduction

Feared, revered, worshipped…the pressure washer has been a stalwart of the post-urban sprawl lexicon since its invention (either 1950 or 1927, depending on whether you are a Karcherite or evangelist of Ofeldt's Jenny). Its function singular but its purposes limitless, it takes any task placed before it and splinters it under the crushing weight of determination and will. It is the Rocky of home improvement/home maintenance tools, powering through its many shortcomings with a steely determination and enlarged aorta the size of a small country, throwing itself headlong at any obstacle until said obstacle yields to its might, defeated in soul and in body.

Pressure washers are simple in theory, but in practice they balance many delicate systems in a symphonic harmony of power. Water goes in, water comes out – but it is in how that water is transformed and pressured that the beauty of their function emerges. To understand the pressure washer is to know the pressure washer, and to know the pressure washer is to love and fear the pressure washer. We will cover how it works, in order that our hearts fill with appreciation and our minds with understanding for this juggernaut's inner machinations.

An instrument of brute force alone, however, she is not. It has the delicate hand of a mother gorilla, ready to rip the faces off any of its enemies but tenderly holding its loved ones close. The pressure washer can tackle many obstacles – we will discuss just how many of these there are. Duct tape it is not, but 1001 uses is a goal within reason for the malleable yet unbreakable will of this angel of aquatic vengeance.

Maintenance of these fearsome beasts is important, and this will be covered in the verses to follow. Like a muscle car of yesteryear, or a moody tiger, they require a little attention to perform and function at their best. Every step will be covered – from first time out of the box, to winter storage, to retirement (although washers don't die, they get rusty and move to the scrap heap, move to the scrap heap), and upgrading. With unfathomable force ripping through each curve and bend of these beautiful monsters, careful and attentive maintenance will keep it alive and at full function much longer. Do not neglect this.

Things go wrong, even in the gnashing anger-filled maws of the pressure washer. With so much violence in so many corners, curves, sinews, and pumps, there is bound to be an entropic failure along some point of the operation. Fear not – we will troubleshoot basic and common stalls in operation, triaging them and repairing to get our humble giants back doing what they do best – fomenting and spreading the germ of carnage and punitive destruction.

Finally, we look to the future. A future where the cleansing chaos of pressure washers brings us a clean slate, a new tablet upon which we forge our worlds. It is in this that the mighty washer finds its spirit, its soul, its purpose. It wipes cleans our sins, that we may start anew and again stumble down the path of patio righteousness.

The pressure washer is not just a tool. It is not just a placeholder in your garage or shed, occupying real estate that would be better served housing a leaf blower. It is a powerful partner, a purring Cerberus at your beck and call. Honor it, treat it as if it was your child, and soon it will shine as you do. Get thine shine on.

The tasks ahead may seem daunting. They may appear to be too much for one person to tackle alone. With *affirmative thought* and your pressure washer at your side, you needn't worry about the difficulty. It's dangerous to go alone. With your friend at your side, you won't have to.

How They Work

In the time before man, before towns and lands,
Rain and harsh water smashed rocks into sand;
A mighty brute force, a mighty wave crests
Spewing foam, salt, and death, to the right and left…

The power of the sea is unrivaled. It withers mountains, feeds the sky, swallows cities and towns whole, claims souls at will and whim. Its force is all-encompassing, ubiquitous like air, but precise like a knife.

It is the pressure washer that carries this mighty lineage from its ancient forebear – not the squirt gun, not the proud dam, but the pressure washer. As sailors of yesteryear feared the deep blue's might and mercurial whim, so should we all be careful with the pressure washer. They are a delicate dance of physics, engineering, and soul.

Pressure washers are simple. The theory is sound. A water intake tube or pipe takes in water from a source – a tank, a faucet or hose, etc. – and using a compressor, fires it out of the other end at a pressure exceeding 700-750 PSI (and reaching over 25,000 PSI in some industrial applications!). Easy, right? Sort of.

    Daybreak – the sun's tendrils stretch forth
    strangling, mangling, enveloping the timid darkness –
    first a little, then a lot, it pulls itself up,
    and with a heave it begins its lazy climb.
    You begin yours too – first out of the bed,
    down the stairs, ginger and slow,
    a yawn and a belly scratch as half-hearted hello.

    The sun greets you gently, tickles the skin.

    Lest you fear, the systems are simple –
    not unlike a friendship, where quiet brings comfort
    and company alone is joy enough,
    where a slow evening, back to the world,
    grin to the fire, and fingers curled
    around a beverage, words and thoughts sparing,
    your cares and worries melt with the timber.
    Water goes in and comes out. That's it.

    An intake hose fills up the water tank.
    This is hooked up to a faucet, an outside garden hose,
    from anywhere a stream of water flows.
    This water goes through a compressor.
    Like the forge of Hephaestus, tempering the strongest steel
    to his exacting, precise whim, each edge – just kidding,
    we're not doing that –
    but there is a compressor, from which comes the pressure.

[Pressure is found through the following equation:
P = rgh; P is pressure, r is density, g is gravitational constant,
(9.806 meters/second squared, of course)
and h is the height of the fluid column.
This physics lesson is not needless.
Compressors, they work to make the volume much smaller.
Density's made of mass over volume.
Smaller the volume, more dense it is.
This makes the pressure skyrocket up real quick.
Compressors, they come in either gas or electric,
using pistons or rotors to raise up the pressure.]

The water's compressed, maybe mixed with soap,
detergents, other cleaners of that scope,
and high-pressure tubing delivers it out.
Many have spray tips that spread water differently,
fan tips or straight blades,
or larger cone-shaped wide area sprays.
Some have just one pressure, some can adjust,
with hand levers or other ways to create thrust.
When power goes off, so too does compression,
and water inside limply falls in depression.

    It is a simplistic concept – take water in, raise its pressure, and spit it back out. The issue does not lie in theory, but the chaos and intrinsic danger in handling high-pressure fluids in tight spaces. We will go over maintenance and safety in future sections, but do be cautious at all times about the dangerous aspect of what we are doing.

The pressure washer's simplicity and ease of operation lends itself to significantly wide swaths of utility. We will now go over the range of uses it has.

Uses

The times we live in are tough. Political strain is at an all time high. Poverty is an unshakeable and seemingly immutable facet of society, or at least one that we don't seem prepared to take the steps to eradicate. It is rare to find something that can help in multiple ways – it seems all our problems have one specific, optimized, expensive solution. The pressure washer is here to smash that model in its pretentious, lofty jaw.

Limitless. Boundless. Without border, without boundary, without strangulating encapsulation. This is the scope of uses our friend the pressure washer holds.

> Again, does the dawn stretch its rosy fingers forth.
> (This is when the author reminds you he has a classics degree! LOL)
> As daybreak peeks through, a welcome guest,
> and sets itself at the table, waiting for a plate -
> what's for breakfast today? Pancakes?
> Love pancakes! I'll have some! -
> and chattering away the morning, laughs and smiles
> and love, each breath it takes warming the house,
> until it is time for its next stop, to visit the next home,

fond farewells and an embrace that sticks with you
- an embrace that lasts a whole day.

The list sits on the table.

As the tepid legume stew courses through capillaries,
carrying vigor, virtue, vivacity,
stirring the soul with a delicate wrist flick,
each swirl, practiced and precise,
ripples in the pond,
the list beckons,
a siren call of suburban sagacity,
ancient wisdom in each stroke of the $0.45 Bic.

"Mow lawn" – a simple command, a simple concept,
understood by child and adult alike.
Pets know to stay wide of the roaring blade,
the loud murder box spreading death and destruction.

Yet eons of knowledge go into this deed.
The wisdom of the first to grow,
raise a lawn as their own,
nurture and guide it as if it was a child,
and the first to trim,
smooth, even ripples of green,
and the first lawn mower,
later made strong with an engine,
souls of many horses encapsulated within,
lending their numinous power for our use.
Should we bag, or should we mulch?
Is the soil pH too low or too much?

Water early, or water late?
The ages have answered these for us.

Yet, the gods recoil in fear.
Had they answered all our lawn questions?
Are we, the awestruck masses, without any will?
No! We have taken back fire from their fold.
With the pressure washer, we harness their strength -
their rules and their laws we flout with offense.
We have taken their tools – water, and air,
and bent them to our will, our whims, our cares.
Each item in the shed has its role and its niche -
but the pressure washer, it is ours, and we do what we wish.

Most known for its skill with the siding of houses,
the pressure washer blasts away the scum of yesteryear.
In a life, we are human, we can't help but gather
all sorts of buildup, grime, flotsam,
despite our aim to do well, it sits on our skin,
- that's where the pressure washer comes in -
a rejuvenating bath for the vinyl siding,
our inner selves again borne to the world, shining.

But lo!
Hold on; wait a minute!
Y'all thought I was finished??
The stains of existence permeate all we own,
all that we interact with, all that we know,
the pressure washer grins with a greedy demeanor,
there's SOMETHING in your life that could be cleaner.

Decks, patios, walkways made of hardy brick?
A 45 degree spray angle should do the trick
1 and a half feet above it you'll spray,
blasting gunk forward and out of the way.

Patio furniture? Lower the strength -
unless shards of wicker or plastic
deep in the buttocks, a self-flagellation
give you joy -
and a summer's stains gone, from your chair and your bench.

You have car ramps? You're in luck -
dragging the detritus of the world home daily,
with its horrors and nightmares
caught in each crevice and crack of the car,
it is a solemn duty to bear the world's burdens -
but you must not let it accumulate under your truck.
Lower the strength, choose a wide fan tip,
and spray, spray, spray, jealousy of the dealership
at your masterful stroke, even and true,
now the wheel wells, go ahead, get them too,
the undercarriage spewing brown-black goo,
watch that you don't get any on you.

Ball stuck in a tree? Pressure washer.
Driveway dirty? Pressure washer.
Did winter, so cruel,
throw six months of gruel,
on the side of the pool? Pressure washer.
Chopping up wood, and your axe, it has failed,
your saws left toothless, your chainsaw has bailed?

Pressure washer.
Violence is wrong, but if the time comes along,
when one, heavens forbid, comes to do wrong,
pressure washer will have them singing a new song.

Be mindful of soap! If the project needs none –
whether wildlife, or surfaces sensitive under sun,
if there's no need for soap, leave that step undone!

Honor its work, its sacrifice,
its sweat and its blood.
Use it for good, use it for right,
use it with honor.
Treat it with dignity.

Maintenance

It is a roaring, growling mass of tubes, water, and sheer anger. Keeping these fine-tuned beasts in order is an important and solemn task; with rigorous maintenance comes long life, and with long life comes joy and utility. Most of what follows is simple – a minute here, a minute there, and your pressure washer will live long and healthy.

> It sets low and long, does the sun,
> dragging feet, asking for a few minutes,
> savoring each last bite of the afternoon.
> Your day is done, however. The list defeated.
> It is time to stable the mare,
> lead the cows back from pasture,
> wrap up a day sealed in sweat and accomplishment.
>
> First, let it cool. Then shut the water.
> Its lifeblood interrupted, the pressure washer,
> ready for sleep 'til time beckons again,
> is ready to be retired for the evening – or for more.
>
> Drain anything left in the tank – soap, water,
> etc – squeeze the trigger or lever…squeeze harder…
> and when you're sure it is empty, squeeze once again.
> You've released the pressure, given it respite.
> Disconnect the hose from the spray gun,

holster the dragon's furious maw,
and give one last look for a drop.

Lulled now to sleep, the washer there lies,
dreaming of flying debris, and clear-blue skies,
its next call to action a gleam in its eye.

If sun's set is early? If winter, she comes,
with her destructive and so-wicked tongue,
hibernation is key. Do follow these steps,
and washer stands, a sentinel of the shed,
when spring breaks it is ready to raise hell again.
Disconnect all tubes – as cold and thaw come,
expanding and contracting can rip small holes in the rubber;
not unlike a mosquito, a pinch and a poke,
and a flight to the next unwitting host,
yet in one bite can be a deadly disease,
one prick felling the strongest to their knees.
Give hoses room to grow and to shrink
so that the contractions don't give armor a chink.

Repair

Despite your best efforts, your most valiant and determined protections, there will be times when the pressure washer fails. Whether random luck, entropy, the agency of chaos, or misuse, you will need to know how to repair and replace certain parts to maintain its longevity. A monster of this ferocity, this force, this sheer energy sometimes exceeds its shell, simply cobbled together by us mortals. We know not how to harness its strength. Our yoke is but paper and twine before its glorious violence. Yet we must learn to repair it, for without it the pressure washer's gifts are but naught.

Do not neglect this. Do not skip this and give up on your washer, replacing it on a whim or at your fancy. It deserves better.

> The crook in his back, a slope of burden.
> The sag of his jowl, time's weight hanging down.
> A crack and a howl, in each tired joint.
> Yet the work continues.
>
> Your washer is fierce (no Sasha) but strong;
> yet once every while, something does go wrong.

It does not roar, it does not shout,
it simply lays catatonic and dead.
Don't fret! Check the spark plug.
Check the carburetor. Ignition coil?
Before these, do save yourself the toil -
...does the washer need gas or oil?

Does it start, then under the weight
of this earth does it buckle and die?
Air problems are my guess;
it is the carburetor that we shall address.
Try to unclog it - no luck? Take it for repair.
Check the pipes for no leaks of air.
Fuel filter might clog - leave sitting the gas,
and it will gum up, new fuel will not pass.
Replace or clean it; it will wake up anew.
If electric: components may be shorted,
power should be aborted,
and to a mechanic this should be reported.

It starts but runs choppy? Carb or air filter.
Off kilter, clogged up, or simply unclean -
take care of these, and smooth running'll be seen.

Is pressure down? Check tubes for a leak.
Water source still flowing at the desired peak?
Compressor sound normal? Checked the pump seals?
Replacing's not hard - unhook flex pipes and place.
If this persists, pump issues abound.
With a frown and a sigh, it's time to rebuild it;
if you cannot, an expert will forge it for you.

A phoenix risen to spread cleansing fire anew.

Soap injection not working? Check the filter
of the spray tip. Or the injector - is the tank filled?
Any suds or trapped solids gumming the works?

Water leakage? Check intake. Check pipes for a leak.
That item - replace it, it won't take a week,
then you're free to return to your sacred duty.

With head bent and eyes low, he returns to his work,
with a sigh and a groan and a practice-fed smirk;
maintaining his vigor as age spins its web
has been hard, but the alternative is that he'd be dead.
For some, that's ok, for him it is not.

Would that he keep strength and spirits aloft!

What's Next

Cassandra rests her wary eye forward, outward, onward. The earth is dying, she portends. We stand slack-jawed in ignorance. It will not be the pressure washer to save us. We should, no, we must learn to harness pressure washer's strengths for energy, for power, for survival. It may be our only hope.

> rivverun, past Eve and Adam's,
> from swerve of shore to bend of bay,
> brings us by a commodius vicus of recirculation
> back to Howth Castle and the environment…

> Up, she asks, look up, at the clouds -
> do you see it? It's an elephant.
> Elephants never forget, she says.
> Neither do I, she says.

> Can you spot me $100? I'm short on rent this month.
> Of course, she says. Of course.
> I'll pay you back in due course, I'm paid Friday.
> Whenever, she says, when you can is ok.

> I'm stuck late at work today, sorry, I sigh.
> That's fine! an understanding smile
> shines through the text message.
> When you can leave let me know,
> I'll have dinner ready!

I'll be pretty late - 1 or 2 in the morning,
don't wait up, please, takeout we're ordering.
Okay, she replies,
if that changes, tell me or I'll be snoring!

'When you can' never came. And we bear the blame,
with an earth ready to replant and re-seed and replow,
A cycle of ages, a cycle we wrought.
Pressure washer, our aegis, is worth but naught.

Or is it? Can it be? It is our savior?
Will its force, its will, bring us from perdition?
Hydroelectricity. It powers so much,
can salt water & pressure carry charges over distance?
Is this our solution, aqueducts of power?
Elon Musk hmu, link in the bio.

The sun, she shines bright, regardless of day,
with no care, no concern, for our wants or our sway,
we must take its strength and bend it our way.
Let no pressure washer draw from the fossils of eld,
no gas, no oil, no coal, our earth is not well.

Can we share aqueous bounty with others abroad?
Under-ocean tunnels that lay down broad,
bringing water to those who go without,
powered by pressure, fighting the drought.

No matter the problem, no matter the issue:
Pressure Washer should be part of the solution.
We took nature, its laws, and bent them to us.

Now we must repay in kind for breaking its trust.
With the tool of offense we cleanse and we wring:
if we don't?
We'll be too dead to pressure wash anything.

The End

Thank you for reading. Please check out my other works:

Unf*ck Your Life: Habits to Hack Your Day

https://www.amazon.com/dp/B071J5S6WZ

disbelief // moving on

https://www.amazon.com/dp/B06XD9ZJ5H

The Young Hope

https://www.amazon.com/dp/B06X3ZQT2H

The Big Picture: The Power of Affirmative Thought

https://www.amazon.com/dp/B01N25U8Y6

Made in the USA
Middletown, DE
05 January 2022